First World War
and Army of Occupation
War Diary
France, Belgium and Germany

14 DIVISION
Divisional Troops
Royal Army Medical Corps
Divisional Field Ambulance Workshop Unit
13 May 1915 - 31 March 1916

WO95/1892/3

The Naval & Military Press Ltd
www.nmarchive.com
Published in association with The National Archives

Published by

The Naval & Military Press Ltd

Unit 10 Ridgewood Industrial Park,

Uckfield, East Sussex,

TN22 5QE England

Tel: +44 (0) 1825 749494

www.naval-military-press.com

www.nmarchive.com

This diary has been reprinted in facsimile from the original. Any imperfections are inevitably reproduced and the quality may fall short of modern type and cartographic standards.

© Crown Copyright
Images reproduced by permission of The National Archives, London, England, 2015.

Contents

Document type	Place/Title	Date From	Date To
Heading	1892/3		
Heading	14th Division 14th Fd Amb Workshop Unit. May 1915-Mar 1916		
Heading	14th Div. 14th 7 A.W.V. Vol. 1,2,3,4,5		
Heading	War Diary Of O.C. 14th Divl. F.A.W.U. From May 13th 1915 to May 31st 1915 (Volume 1.)		
War Diary	Rouen	13/05/1915	14/05/1915
War Diary	Neufchatel	15/05/1915	15/05/1915
War Diary	Abbeville	16/05/1915	16/05/1915
War Diary	St Omer.	17/05/1915	22/05/1915
War Diary	Watten	23/05/1915	26/05/1915
War Diary	Rubrouck	27/05/1915	27/05/1915
War Diary	St Sylvestre Cappel.	28/05/1915	30/05/1915
War Diary	Westoutre	31/05/1915	31/05/1915
Heading	War Diary Of O.C. 14th Divl. F.A.W.U. From June 1st 1915 to June 30th 1915 (Volume 2)		
War Diary	Westoutre	01/06/1915	13/06/1915
War Diary	Hilhoek	14/06/1915	30/06/1915
Heading	War Diary Of O.C. 14th Divl. F.A.W.U. MT. A.S.C. From July 1st 1915 To July 31st 1915 (Volume.3)		
War Diary	Hilhoek	01/07/1915	21/07/1915
Miscellaneous			
War Diary	Hilhoek	22/07/1915	25/07/1915
War Diary	Ate Jean	26/07/1915	31/07/1915
Heading	War Diary Of O.C. 14th Divl. F.A.W.U. MT. A.S.C. From August 1st 1915 to August 31st 1915 (Volume 4)		
War Diary	St. Jean (Waton)	01/08/1915	12/08/1915
War Diary	St. Jean	13/08/1915	31/08/1915
Heading	War Diary Of O.C. 14th Divl. F.A.W.U. MT. A.S.C. From 1st Sept. 1915 to 30th Sept 1915 (Volume 5)		
War Diary	St. Jean (Waton)	01/09/1915	30/09/1915
Heading	14th Division 14th F.A.W.U. Vol. 6 Oct 15		
Heading	War Diary Of O.C. 14th Divl. F.A.W.U. MT A.S.C. From Oct 1st 1915 To Oct 31st 1915 (Volume 6)		
War Diary	St Jean Waton	01/10/1915	31/10/1915
Miscellaneous	14th Division 14th F.A.W.U. Vol 7 Nov 15		
Heading	War Diary Of O.C. 14th Divl. F.A.W.U. MT.A.S.C. From Nov 1st 1915 To Nov 30th 1915 (Volume 7)		
War Diary	St. Jean (Waton)	01/11/1915	30/11/1915
Heading	14th Div 14th F.A.W.U. Vol. 8 December 1915		
Heading	War Diary Of O.C. 14th Divl. F.A.W.U. MT. A.S.C. From Dec 1st 1915 To Dec 31st 1915 (Volume 8)		
War Diary	St. Jean (Waton)	01/12/1915	31/12/1915
Miscellaneous	Nominal Roll of the 14th Divl F.A.W.U.	19/12/1915	19/12/1915
Heading	12th F.A.W.U Vol. 9 Jan 1916		
Heading	War Diary Of O.C. 14th Divl. F.A.W.U. MT. A.S.C. From Jan 1st 1916-To Jan 31st 1916 (Volume 9)		
War Diary	St. Jean Waton	01/01/1916	31/01/1916
Heading	14th F.A.W.U. Vol 10 Feb 1916 March 1916		

Heading	War Diary Of O.C. 14th Divl. F.A.W.U. MT. A.S.C. From Feb. 1st 1916 To Feb. 29th 1916 (Volume 10)		
War Diary	St. Jean (Waton)	01/02/1916	12/02/1916
War Diary	Esquelbecq	13/02/1916	20/02/1916
War Diary	Flesselles	21/02/1916	25/02/1916
War Diary	Doullens	26/02/1916	29/02/1916
Heading	War Diary Of O.C. 14th Divl. F.A.W.U. MT. A.S.C. From March 1st 1916 To March 31st 1916 (Volume II)		
War Diary	Doullens	01/03/1916	01/03/1916
War Diary	Barly	02/03/1916	07/03/1916
War Diary	Fosseux	08/03/1916	19/03/1916
War Diary	Wanquetin	20/03/1916	31/03/1916

1892/3

14TH DIVISION

14TH FD AMB WORKSHOP UNIT.

MAY 1915 - MAR 1916

14. K. J. a. W. V.
fol.: 1, 2, 3, 4, 5.

131/7936

Mai 15
Mai 16

1915

Confidential.

War Diary

of

O. C. 14th Divl. F. A. W. U.
MT. A. S. C.

From May. 13th 1915 to May 31st 1915.

(Volume . 1.)

Army Form C. 2118.

WAR DIARY
or
INTELLIGENCE SUMMARY.
(Erase heading not required.)

Instructions regarding War Diaries and Intelligence Summaries are contained in F. S. Regs., Part II. and the Staff Manual respectively. Title pages will be prepared in manuscript.

Place	Date	Hour	Summary of Events and Information	Remarks and references to Appendices
Rouen	May 13th		Disembarked at Rouen at 4pm. 1 Officer 67 men 25 Vehicles 3 M/cycles. Parked Vehicles	1SNS
"	14		2 men to Base M.T. Depot. Repaired damage to lorry caused in embarking.	1SNS
Neufchatel	15		Received orders from A.D.T. at 4pm. to proceed to Neufchatel en route for Abbeville. Marched out at 4.30 to Neufchatel and parked for the night.	1SNS
Abbeville	16		8.30 marched out. Arrived Abbeville 12 noon & proceeded to rest camp. Received orders from D.A.Q.M.G. Adv Base to proceed to 25 Omer at 9 am. 17-5-15.	1SNS
	17.		Marched out 9 am. arrived at Omer 3.30 pm. and parked Vehicles	1SNS
St Omer	18		1 Gift Ambulance & 2 men to 1st Cav. Div. FAWU. Found all Sunbeam front spring attachments working loose. Replaced all road spring packings with leather, fitted distance pieces between spring clips and castellated all spring clip nuts & fitted split pins.	1SNS
"	19		1 Gift Ambulance & 2 men to 25th Fd. Amb. 1 Gift Ambulance & 2 men to 10th Fd Amb. 1 Gift Ambulance and 2 men to 27th Divn ----- 1 Ambulance & 2 men from 25th Fd Amb. 1 Ambulance & 2 men from 10th Fd Amb. 1 Ambulance & 2 men from 27th Divn	1SNS
"	20		Despatched 6 Ambulances 1 M/cycle & 13 men to join 42nd Field Ambulance at Bolgle.	1SNS
"	21		Unit inspected by D.T. Staff	1SNS
"	22.		Overhauled Ambulance received from 27th Divn. Received orders for A.D.M.S. 14th Divn to proceed to Watten on 23-5-15	1SNS

WAR DIARY
or
INTELLIGENCE SUMMARY.
(Erase heading not required.)

Army Form C. 2118.

Place	Date	Hour	Summary of Events and Information	Remarks and references to Appendices
	May			
Watten	23		Marched out at 9 am. Arrived Watten 9.50am and parked outside camping ground while making up road at entrance to somewhat boggy farmyard.	SEA.
"	24		Made standing for lorries. Overhauled cars. Received from 10th Fd Ambulance.	SEA.
"	25		Despatched 7. Ambulance 1 m/cycle 15 men to 43rd Field ambulance at Lederzeele. Handed over 7 Ambulances 1 m/cycle 15 men to 44th Field Ambulance at Watten.	SEA.
"	26		1. Ambulance & 2 men from 104th Field amb. Received orders from D.H.Q. to march out on 27-5-15.	SEA.
Rubrouck	27.		Marched out at 12.50 in rear of Division to Rubrouck but found it necessary to Rail to allow Divn to get ahead before proceeding owing to overheating of the lorries due to the slow speed. Received orders from D.H.Q. to march out on 28-5-15 to Steenvoorde.	SEA.
Rubr: St Sylvestre Cappel.	28		Marched out at 8.20 in rear of Divn. Found it necessary to make three halts of 1 hour each to allow divn to get ahead. Arrived Steenvoorde & received orders from D.H.Q. to go to St Sylvestre Cappel. Arrived St Sylvestre Cappel & parked vehicles on Railway siding. Handed over 1. Ambulance & 2 men to 42nd Field ambulance.	SEA. SEA. SEA.
"	29		Overhauled Ambulance. Received from 25th Fd. Ambulance.	SEA.
"	30		Received orders from D.H.Q. to march at a.31st to Westoutre.	SEA.
Westoutre	31		Marched out 10am to Westoutre & parked vehicles. Built long standings & latrines.	SEA.

CONFIDENTIAL.

War Diary
of.

O.C. 14th Divl. F.A.W.U.
MT. A.S.C.

From June 1st 1915 to June 30th 1915.

(Volume 2)

Army Form C. 21

WAR DIARY
or
INTELLIGENCE SUMMARY.
(Erase heading not required.)

Instructions regarding War Diaries and Intelligence Summaries are contained in F. S. Regs., Part II. and the Staff Manual respectively. Title pages will be prepared in manuscript.

Place	Date	Hour	Summary of Events and Information	Remarks and references to Appendices
Meatoutre	June 1.		Find that the rear dumb irons of 16th Sunbeam Ambulances are splitting owing to faulty design of half elliptic spring & shackle, am rolling up the end of springs 3/4" on all this model of Sunbeam Ambulance to cure this fault, the springs should have been made shorter & with less camber.	MS. MS.
"	2.		3 cars for alteration to springs.	MS
"	3		3 " " " & 1 Daimler with gearbox trouble.	MS
"	4		1 car in Workshop for repair	MS
"	5		1 " " "	MS
"	6		2 " " "	MS
"	7		1 car in collision with Lorry, Front axle & dumb iron bent & repairs to radiator	MS
"	8		2 Cars in Workshop for repair	MS
"	9		1 car awaiting of one parts for gearbox.	MS
"	10		1 car in for repair & 1 awaiting of spare parts	MS
"	11 & 12		1 " " " " "	MS
"	13		Received orders from A.D.M.S. to march on 14-6-15 to Hillock at 11.30.	MS.
Hillock	14		Marched out at 11.30 to Hillock. Roads very congested by rest of Division. Daimler in tow with Arrived Hillock 1.10 pm. & made camp in grass field made long standing & latrines.	MS.

1577 Wt.W10791/1773 500,000 1/15 D. D. & L. A.D.S.S./Forms/C. 2118.

Army Form C. 2118.

WAR DIARY
or
INTELLIGENCE SUMMARY.
(Erase heading not required.)

Instructions regarding War Diaries and Intelligence Summaries are contained in F. S. Regs., Part II. and the Staff Manual respectively. Title pages will be prepared in manuscript.

Place	Date	Hour	Summary of Events and Information	Remarks and references to Appendices
Hillock	June 15		1 car awaiting spare parts. Built incinerator, grease trap, bivouacs & cookhouse.	1803
"	16		"	1803
"	17		2 cars for repair.	1803
"	18		" & 1 Motor Cart.	1803
"	19		3 "	1803
"	20		2 "	1803
"	21		1 " I find Sunbeam Springs are tempered too hard for these bad roads & are.	1803
"	22		2 "	1803
"	23		1 "	1803
"	24-25		No cars in for repair. Took down & cleaned engine of light lorry.	1803
"	26		1 Car for repair	1803
"	27		4 "	1803
"	28		2 "	1803
"	29		3 "	1803
"	30		2 " Am having a great deal of trouble with Sunbeam springs breaking but find that springs made up in this workshop & tempered soft are quite satisfactory. Am replacing Sunbeam made springs with these as the former break.	1803

1577 Wt.W.10791/1773 500,000 1/15 D. D. & L.   A.D.S.S./Forms/C. 2118.

Confidential

War Diary
of.

O. C. 14th Divl. F. A. W. U.
MT. A. S. C.

From July 1st 1915 To July 31st 1915

(Volume 3)

Army Form C. 2118.

WAR DIARY
or
INTELLIGENCE SUMMARY.
(Erase heading not required.)

Instructions regarding War Diaries and Intelligence Summaries are contained in F. S. Regs., Part II. and the Staff Manual respectively. Title pages will be prepared in manuscript.

Place	Date	Hour	Summary of Events and Information	Remarks and references to Appendices
Hillock	July 1st		1 car in for repair.	SUB
"	2		3 Ambulances & 6 men from No 1 M.A.C. sent in exchange for 3 Fd Ambulances. Overhauled these & found rear springs weak & back axles striking the spring brackets on the frame. Corrected springing. I find this fault on all 12-16 Sunbeam Ambulances of 1914 make and overcome it by placing a stiffening plate under the scroll plate of the top ½ elliptic spring & hanging it round into the eye. Placing a wedge between the spring & frame bracket so as to tilt the back end of the spring downwards & putting an extra plate in the ½ elliptic spring. This enables the car to carry its full load over bad roads without trouble.	SUB
"	3		Completed work on Ambulances received yesterday & despatched on each to 42nd, 43rd & 44th Fd Ambulances. Withdrew 1 Ford Ambulance from each Fd Amb.	SUB
"	4		3 Fd Ambulances to No 1 M.A.C. 2 cars to repair.	SUB
"	5		2 cars to repair.	SUB
"	6		1 " " "	SUB
"	7		1 " " "	SUB
"	8		2 " " " One Ambulance in collision with a lorry & ran into ditch, sent out	SUB

Army Form C. 2118.

WAR DIARY
or
INTELLIGENCE SUMMARY.
(Erase heading not required.)

Instructions regarding War Diaries and Intelligence Summaries are contained in F. S. Regs., Part II. and the Staff Manual respectively. Title pages will be prepared in manuscript.

Place	Date	Hour	Summary of Events and Information	Remarks and references to Appendices
Hillock	July 8th		Breakdown gang & towed it in. Found damage too extensive for local repair and despatched car & two drivers to G.H.Q. Repair Shops.	MSS.
"	9		no cars for repair	MSS.
"	10	1 "	" " "	MSS.
"	11	1 "	" " "	MSS.
"	12	2 "	" " "	MSS.
"	13	2 "	Am experiencing great delay in obtaining spare parts from Adv. M.T. Depot.	MSS.
"	14	3 "	" " "	MSS.
"	15	6 "	Gd Ambulance ditched at Vlamertinghe & spring broken & axle bent; towed in.	MSS.
"	16	4 "	" " "	MSS.
"	17	1 "	" " "	MSS.
"	18	2 "	" " "	MSS.
"	19	3 "	" " "	MSS.
"	20	3 "	" " "	MSS.
"	21	4 "	Gd Ambulance in collision with two other Ambulances of No. 5 M.A.C. Considerable damage done, axle & steering & wheels damaged & frame bent & broken in 2 places.	MSS.

2.

c. will be evacuated to the Corps Cage, B.19.c.7.4. by mounted escort supplied by XVIII Corps for this purpose.

4. PERSONNEL.

a. All officers detailed for duties in connection with Straggler Posts, Prisoners' Cages, etc. will report to the A.P.M. 11th Division at the Western end of BRIDGE 4 at 8 p.m. on Oct. 2nd for instructions.

b. All personnel detailed for duties in connection with Straggler Posts, Prisoners Cages, etc. will move to their positions at Zero minus 12 hours. They will carry the unconsumed portion of the day's ration and rations for the two following days. They will return to their units automatically at Zero plus 48 hours.

5. TRAFFIC CONTROL.

a. Traffic Circuit Map, Forward Area has been issued to all concerned under 11th Division. I.G. No. 56 and 86/Q/25.
b. Control Posts will be established at :-
   (a). C.25.a.3.7.
   (b). C.25.a.5.8.
   (c). C.25.a.8.9.
   (d). C.19.d.9.2.
   (e). C.20.c.5.1.   (g.) C.10.c.1.4.
   (f). C.19.c.0.6.

Traffic Control Patrol between BRIDGE 4, ZOUAVE VILLA. HAMMONDS CORNER.

c. All traffic will keep strictly to circuits. In the event of it becoming necessary to close any circuit, instructions will be issued to Control Posts who will effect the necessary deviations.

6. CASUALTIES.

will be reported as ordered in Standing Orders for Battle, Appendix 12.

7. BURIALS.

Cemeteries have been established at :-
U.30.c.6.5.   C. 5.d.3.2.   C. 8.b.1.8.
C. 5.b.9.9.   C. 5.d.4.4.   C. 9.d.9.2.
U.30.a.7.4.   C. 6.a.1.1.   C.14.c.8.8.

The dead should be buried in recognized cemeteries only. It is however often necessary for sanitary reasons that they should be buried by troops practically in the firing line. When this is done, care should be taken that all details of men so buried and the exact sites are reported by Brigades to the Divisional Burial Officer.

8. AREAS AND ACCOMMODATION.

a. List of Area Commandants from the Canal inclusive Westwards has been issued to all concerned under 11th Division Administrative Instructions No. 24.

b. Instructions with regard to accommodation East of the Canal have been issued under 11th Division G.S.843 dated 25/9/17, G.S.889 D/28/9/17 and G.S.904 D/29/9/17.

The Area Commandant Forward Area is Lieut. G.F. BROWN, 6th E. York. Regt. Dug-out 194 Canal Bank, West. He is in communication with Advanced Divisional Exchange.

c. Burial Officer and party will evacuate present accommodation at FERDINAND FARM on Oct. 1st. Further accommodation will be allotted later.

d. Area Comdts. from CANAL BANK Westwards have been notified of all moves up to October 3rd inclusive. Advanced parties will report to Area Comdts. at least 1 hour in advance of the Main Body.

c./

Army Form C. 2118.

WAR DIARY
or
INTELLIGENCE SUMMARY.
(Erase heading not required.)

Instructions regarding War Diaries and Intelligence Summaries are contained in F. S. Regs., Part II. and the Staff Manual respectively. Title pages will be prepared in manuscript.

Place	Date	Hour	Summary of Events and Information	Remarks and references to Appendices
Hillock	July 22		4 Cars in for repair	SES
"	23		5 " " " "	SES
"	24		3 " " " "	SES
"	25		2 " " " "	SES
St Jean	26		Received orders from DHQ to march out on 26-7-15 to St Jean (Walton). Marched out 12 noon to St Jean - tia Dirugen (Walton) Arrived 12.30 pm. One car in tow (under repair). Erected latrines & incinerator & arranged shelter for working under. Personnel went into billets. Net day some trouble was experienced in getting lorries out of field in which they were parked.	SES
"	27		1 car under repair	SES
"	28		1 Ambulance & 2 drivers from No 1 M.A.C. to replace casualty of 8th inst. 2 cars for repair.	SES
"	29		3 cars for repair. One Ambulance in collision with a tree owing to breakage of steering arm + not of car very badly damaged & beyond local repair. Towed it to Railhead & sent to Paris repair shop.	SES
"	30		2 cars for repair. 1 Ambulance & 2 drivers from No 1 M.A.C. to replace yesterdays casualty	SES
"	31		6 cars for repair. Very busy. Heavy casualties last night & roads between Ypres districts in very bad condition. Several Ambulances caught under shrapnel fire & bodies damaged. all the cars today have broken springs.	SES

Confidential

War Diary
of
O.C. 14th Divl. F.A.W.U.
MT. A.S.C.

From August 1st 1915 to August 31st 1915

(Volume 4)

Army Form C. 2118.

WAR DIARY
or
INTELLIGENCE SUMMARY.
(Erase heading not required.)

Instructions regarding War Diaries and Intelligence Summaries are contained in F. S. Regs., Part II. and the Staff Manual respectively. Title pages will be prepared in manuscript.

Place	Date	Hour	Summary of Events and Information	Remarks and references to Appendices
Nr Ypres (Walton)	August 1		8 cars in for repair. This makes 14 cars in two days all with broken & damaged springs due to overloading on the bad road from Ypres to donelling wood did post, most of the casualties are now evacuated but I have written ADMS requesting that the Ambulances be not sent so far forward as the last part of the road is not practicable further. Several of the cars in try have suffered from shell fire.	MS
"	2		3 cars in for repair	MS
"	3		5 " " " "	MS
"	4		3 " " " "	MS
"	5		6 " " " "	MS
"	6		3 " " " "	MS
"	7		3 " " " "	MS
"	8		5 " " " "	MS
"	9		4 " " " " 1 Fitter evacuated sick to C.C.S.	MS
"	10		3 " " " "	MS
"	11		1 " " " "	MS
"	12		3 " " " "	MS

Army Form C. 2118.

WAR DIARY
or
INTELLIGENCE SUMMARY.
(Erase heading not required.)

Instructions regarding War Diaries and Intelligence Summaries are contained in F. S. Regs., Part II. and the Staff Manual respectively. Title pages will be prepared in manuscript.

Place	Date	Hour	Summary of Events and Information	Remarks and references to Appendices
St Omer	August 13	4	Cars in for repair.	see.
"	14	2	" " " "	see.
"	15	2	" " " "	see.
"	16	2	" " " "	see.
"	17	2	" " " "	see.
"	18	5	" " " "	see.
"	19	5	" " " "	see.
"	20	5	" " " "	see.
"	21	4	" " " "	see.
"	22	4	" " " " 1. Lorry driver evacuated sick to C.C.S.	see.
"	23	5	" " " "	see.
"	24	1	" " " "	see.
"	25	3	" " " " 1. Fitter from Base M.T. Depot.	see.
"	26	2	" " " "	see.
"	27	1	" " " "	see.
"	28	3	" " " "	see.

Army Form C. 2118

WAR DIARY
or
INTELLIGENCE SUMMARY.
(Erase heading not required.)

Instructions regarding War Diaries and Intelligence Summaries are contained in F. S. Regs., Part II. and the Staff Manual respectively. Title pages will be prepared in manuscript.

Place	Date	Hour	Summary of Events and Information	Remarks and references to Appendices
St. Jean	August 29		4 cars in for repair	SEE
	30		6 cars " "	SEE
	31		4 " " "	SEE
			Am experiencing very considerable delay in obtaining spare parts from div. M.T. Depot. Men have consequently to work very late in order to make up spare parts which should be obtained ready to fit.	SEE.

1577 Wt.W10791/1773 500,000 1/15 D. D. & L. A.D.S.S./Forms/C. 2118.

CONFIDENTIAL

War Diary
of
**O. C. 14th Divl. F. A. W. U.
MT. A. S. C.**

From 1st Sept. 1915 to 30th Sept 1915

(Volume 5)

Army Form C. 2118.

WAR DIARY
or
INTELLIGENCE SUMMARY.
(Erase heading not required.)

Instructions regarding War Diaries and Intelligence Summaries are contained in F. S. Regs., Part II. and the Staff Manual respectively. Title pages will be prepared in manuscript.

Place	Date	Hour	Summary of Events and Information	Remarks and references to Appendices
St. Jean (Huts)	Sept. 1.		3 cars in for repair	nes
"	2		3 " " " "	nes
"	3		4 " " " "	nes
"	4		3 " " " "	nes
"	5		7 " " " "	nes
"	6		6 " " " "	nes
"	7		7 " " " "	nes
"	8		6 " " " "	nes
"	9		7 " " " " Roads in and East of Ypres now in very bad state owing to shell fire.	nes
"	10		6 " " " " 1 m/cycle casualty to Supply Column. 19 yards from Supply Column in replacement.	nes
"	11		5 " " " "	nes
"	12		5 " " " "	nes
"	13		5 " " " "	nes
"	14		4 " " " " One car fell into large shell hole in Ypres last night. Tourelli in badly damaged.	nes
"	15		5 " " " " 1 fitter evacuated sick to C.C.S.	nes
"	16		3 " " " "	nes

Army Form C. 2118.

WAR DIARY
or
INTELLIGENCE SUMMARY.
(Erase heading not required.)

Instructions regarding War Diaries and Intelligence Summaries are contained in F. S. Regs., Part II. and the Staff Manual respectively. Title pages will be prepared in manuscript.

Place	Date	Hour	Summary of Events and Information	Remarks and references to Appendices
St Jean (India)	Sept. 17		6 cars in for repair.	see
"	18		4 " " " 6 additional m/cycles drawn from Supply Column for Field Ambulances.	see
"	19		3 " " "	see
"	20		3 " " "	see
"	21		6 " " " Overhauling springs of cars in rear of possible heavy casualties shortly.	see
"	22		4 " " " " " "	see
"	23		7 " " " " " "	see
"	24		5 " " " " " "	see
"	25		4 " " " Attack took place & early this morning all cars out & very busy.	see
"	26		3 " " " 1 car & 2 drivers to G.H.Q. Repair shops with broken backaxle	see
"	27		3 " " " Cars are working very hard but standing up well so far.	see
"	28		7 " " " mostly springs, due to heavy work. 1 Lorry Driver / fitter from Base M.T. Depot.	see
"	29		5 " " "	see
"	30		5 " " "	see

14 ℥ J.A.u.
vol: 6

121/7795

Aug 3

14" W.S.K. Brann

Oct 15

Ct.15

F

(COPY) *original from activity in France*

CONFIDENTIAL

WAR DIARY

OF

O.C. 2nd DIV. F. & W.U.
MT. A.S.C.

From Oct 1st 1905 to Oct 31st 1905

(VOLUME 6)

Army Form C. 2118.

WAR DIARY
or
INTELLIGENCE SUMMARY.
(Erase heading not required.)

Instructions regarding War Diaries and Intelligence Summaries are contained in F. S. Regs., Part II. and the Staff Manual respectively. Title pages will be prepared in manuscript.

Place	Date	Hour	Summary of Events and Information	Remarks and references to Appendices
St Jean Wodon	Oct. 1.		5 cars in for repair	AAA
"	2		4 " " " "	AAA
"	3		3 " " " "	AAA
"	4		3 " " " "	AAA
"	5		4 " " " "	AAA
"	6		3 " " " "	AAA
"	7		3 " " " "	AAA
"	8		7 " " " "	AAA
"	9		7 " " " "	AAA
"	10		5 " " " "	1 Car & 2 drivers from II Army Troops Supply Column to replace casualty of 26/9/15.
"	11		2 " " " "	AAA
"	12		2 " " " "	AAA
"	13		3 " " " "	AAA
"	14		1 " " " "	AAA
"	15		4 " " " "	AAA
"	16		2 " " " "	AAA

Army Form C. 2118.

WAR DIARY
INTELLIGENCE SUMMARY.

(Erase heading not required.)

Place	Date	Hour	Summary of Events and Information	Remarks and references to Appendices
At Jean (Abaton)	Oct 17th	2	Cars in for repair. Made 24 traverses for trench stretchers delivered to 4-3rd Brigade.	
"	18	4	" " " "	
"	19	4	" " " " Built drying room for men's clothes	
"	20	3	" " " "	
"	21	4	" " " " Work is being delayed owing to shortage of Paraffin for cleaning out gearboxes etc.	
"	22	4	" " " "	
"	23	3	" " " "	
"	24	5	" " " "	
"	25	4	" " " "	
"	26	4	" " " "	
"	27	4	" " " "	
"	28	4	" " " " 1. Blacksmith evacuated sick to C.C.S.	
"	29	5	" " " "	
"	30	3	" " " "	
"	31	5	" " " " Experiencing difficulty in carrying out the work properly without paraffin for cleaning parts, practically none obtainable now	

14th Adrain 14 = Fasc. vol 7.

121/7656

Nov 15

CONFIDENTIAL

War Diary
of

O.C. 14th Divl. F.A.W.U.
MT. A.S.C.

From Nov 1st 1915 - To Nov 30th 1915

(Volume 7)

Army Form C. 2118

WAR DIARY
or
INTELLIGENCE SUMMARY.
(Erase heading not required.)

Instructions regarding War Diaries and Intelligence Summaries are contained in F. S. Regs., Part II. and the Staff Manual respectively. Title pages will be prepared in manuscript.

Place	Date	Hour	Summary of Events and Information	Remarks and references to Appendices
St Jean (Wieltje)	Nov. 1	9/pm	2 Cars in for repair. Much rain. Roads getting very bad.	SCS
"	2	9 pm	2 " " " " Obtained bricks & made standings for cars when being worked on & escorts keep man dry.	SCS. SCS
"	3	10 pm	6 " " " " 1 Ambulance & 2 drivers from 2nd Army 1 m/cy to Asst H. Column	SCS
"	4	9 pm	5 " " " " 1 Ambulance & 2 drivers to GHQ for repair.	SCS
"	5	9 pm	4 " " " " & 1 awaiting spare parts from MT Depot. Made 24 Traverses for Royer trench stretcher.	SCS.
"	6	8.30 pm	3 " " " " Roads in very bad condition.	SCS.
"	7	9 pm	3 cars awaiting spare parts. 2 cars ditched at Rest Camp, stripped gear getting out. Other broke fatigue rod bracket.	SCS.
"	8	7.30 pm	3 Cars awaiting spare parts 1. Car for repair. 1 m/cycle & 2 m/cycles & 1 horse ambulance.	SCS.
"	9	9 pm	3 " " " " & 3 Cars 2 1 m/cycle for repair. Owing to lack of protection the steering joints of Ford Ambulances have been wearing out very rapidly since the advent of wet weather. I consider that they should be provided with some form of leather protecting sleeves.	
"	10	10 pm	3 Cars awaiting spare parts & 1 Car & 1 m/cycle for repair. 1 lorry to Hazebrouck for new rear tyres.	SCS. SCS.
"	11	9 pm	2 Cars & 1 m/cycle awaiting spare parts. 3 cars for repair. Wet day.	SCS.
"	12	9.30 pm	2 Cars & 2 m/cycles " " 4 " " Very wet day.	SCS.
"	13	9 pm	2 cars & 2 m/cycles " " 2 " "	SCS.

1577 Wt W10791/1773 500,000 1/15 D. D. & L. A.D.S.S./Forms/C. 2118.

WAR DIARY
or
INTELLIGENCE SUMMARY.
(Erase heading not required.)

Army Form C. 2118

Instructions regarding War Diaries and Intelligence Summaries are contained in F. S. Regs., Part II. and the Staff Manual respectively. Title pages will be prepared in manuscript.

Place	Date	Hour	Summary of Events and Information	Remarks and references to Appendices
Rouen (Station)	Nov.			
	14th	9.30p	2 cars & 2 m/cycles awaiting spare parts. 3 cars for repair. Sharp frost tonight. Am emptying radiators of cars as I am unable to obtain methylated spirit to anti-freeze mixture	ADS
"	15	9 p.m.	2 cars & 2 m/cycles awaiting spare parts. Gu Ambulance in collision, frame badly broken, despatched to Rouen for repairs. 4 cars for repair. Sharp frost tonight.	BCB
"	16	8 p.m.	2 Ambulances to G.H.Q. Repair shops with faulty back axles. 2 m/cycles awaiting spare parts. 2 cars in for repair.	BCB.
"	17	9 p.m.	2 m/cycles awaiting spare parts. 3 cars in for repair.	BCB.
"	18	10 p.m.	1. 9/cycle awaiting spare parts. 5 cars & 1 m/cycle for repair. Sharp frosts every night now. Cannot obtain methylated spirit for radiators of cars.	BCB.
"	19	10.30p	3 Ambulances & 3 drivers from 2nd Army Troops Supply Column to replace casualties of 15th & 16th	BCB.
"	20	9 p.m.	1. m/cycle awaiting spare parts. 4 cars & 1 m/cycle for repair	BCB.
"	21	9 p.m.	1. M/cycle awaiting spare parts. 6 cars in for repair	BCB.
"	22	9 p.m.	1 " " " 3 cars & 1 m/cycle for repair	BCB.
"	23	9.30p	1 " " " 6 cars in for repair	ADS
"	24	10 p.m.	1 " " " 9 cars & 1 m/cycle in for repair	ADS.
"			3 cars & 3 m/cycles in for repair	ADS.

Army Form C. 2118

WAR DIARY
or
INTELLIGENCE SUMMARY.
(Erase heading not required.)

Instructions regarding War Diaries and Intelligence
Summaries are contained in F.S. Regs., Part II.
and the Staff Manual respectively. Title pages
will be prepared in manuscript.

Place	Date	Hour	Summary of Events and Information	Remarks and references to Appendices
St Jean (Italian)	Nov. 25	9 p.m.	1 m/cycle awaiting spare parts. 3 cars in for repair	R.e.B.
"	26	9 p.m.	1 " " " " 6 " " " Snow & frost at night.	R.e.B.
"	27	9 p.m.	1 " " " " 3 cars & 2 m/cycles in for repair. Hard frost. Am still unable to obtain any anti freezing mixture for radiators of cars. 1 man from Base M.T. Depot.	R.e.B.
"	28	9 p.m.	1 m/cycle awaiting spare parts 3 cars & 1 m/cycle in for repair	R.e.B.
"	29	9.30 p.m.	1 " " " " 5 " 2 " " " "	R.e.B.
"	30	8.30 p.m.	1 " " " " 4 " 1 " " " "	B.C.B.

4th P.a.W.V.
Vol: 8

December 1918

CONFIDENTIAL

WAR DIARY
OF
O. C. 14th Div. F. A. W. U.
MT. A. S. C.

From Dec. 1st 1905. To Dec 31st 1905.

(VOLUME. 8)

Army Form C. 2118.

WAR DIARY
or
INTELLIGENCE SUMMARY
(Erase heading not required.)

Instructions regarding War Diaries and Intelligence Summaries are contained in F. S. Regs., Part II. and the Staff Manual respectively. Title pages will be prepared in manuscript.

Place	Date	Hour	Summary of Events and Information	Remarks and references to Appendices
At Yeanangyaung	Dec. 1st	9 p.m.	1 m/cycle awaiting spare parts	Ref.
"	2.	10 p.m.	3 cars & 1 m/cycle in for repair	Ref.
"	3	8.30 p	3 cars for repair. To Pakôkku with light lorry to bring in broken down Ford.	Ref.
"	4	9 p.m.	4 cars & 1 m/cycle in for repair	Ref.
"	5	9 "	4 " " "	Ref.
"	6	9 p.m.	2 " " "	Ref.
"	7	9 p.m.	2 cars for repair	Ref.
"	8	10 p.m.	1 car for repair	Ref.
"	9	9 p.m.	3 cars for repair	Ref.
"	10	9 p.m.	4 cars & 2 m/cycles for repair. 1 lorry to 25th F.A.W.C. 1 lorry for 25th F.A.W.C.	Ref.
"	11	9 p.m.	4 cars & 3 " " "	Ref.
"	12	8.30 p.	5 cars for repair	Ref.
"	13	9 p.m.	1 " " "	Ref.
"	14	10 p.m.	3 cars & 1 m/cycle for repair. Returned camp material in view of coming move.	Ref.
"	15	9 p.m.	7 cars & 1 m/cycle for repair. Returned surplus spare parts to M.T. Depot.	Ref.
"	16	9 p.m.	3 cars for repair. 1 m/cycle to 14th Div. Supply Column.	Ref.

WAR DIARY
or
INTELLIGENCE SUMMARY

(Erase heading not required.)

Army Form C. 2118.

Instructions regarding War Diaries and Intelligence Summaries are contained in F. S. Regs., Part II. and the Staff Manual respectively. Title pages will be prepared in manuscript.

Place	Date	Hour	Summary of Events and Information	Remarks and references to Appendices
St Jean	17	10 p.m.	4 Cars & 2 m/cycles in for repair	R.C.B.
"	18	11 a.m.	2 Cars & 2 m/cycles " " "	R.C.B.
"	19	9 a.m.	3 " " 2 " " " "	"
"	20	10 a.m.	7 " " 1 " " " "	B.C.B.
"	21	9.30 p.m.	2 " " 1 " " " "	"
"	22	8 p.m.	3 Cars & 2 m/cycles " " "	"
"	23	10 p.m.	6 " " 1 " " " "	R.C.B.
"	24	11 p.m.	4 " " 1 " out " "	R.C.B.
"	25	12 p.m.	3 Cars for repair. Took over 20 Ambulances packed up Workshops ready to march out at 7am. Orders received from H.Q. at 7pm to let one move and stand by.	B.C.B.
"	26	9 a.m.	One fitter to 367 M.T. Coy. A.S.C. Received orders from A.D.M.S. to proceed to Havre on 26/12/15. Received orders from H.Q. to cancel orders re. move & returned Cars to Field Ambulances & remade camp. One Ambulance & 2 drivers to 2nd Army Troops Supply Column.	B.C.B.
"	27	9 p.m.	2 Cars for repair. Lorry to Vlamertinghe to tow in a breakdown.	R.C.B.
"	28	11 a.m.	3 Cars & 2 m/cycles for repair. 1 car awaiting spare parts from M.T. Depot.	R.C.B.
"	29	9 a.m.	3 " " 1 " " " "	"
"	30	9 p.m.	4 " " 1 " & 1 Lorry for Repair	"
"	31	8 p.m.	2 " " 1 " " " "	R.C.B.

Nominal Roll of the 14th Divl F.A.W.U.

Number		Rank	Name	Remarks
		Lieut.	B.C. Barton	
M/S	2435	M.S. Sergt.	Carpenter A.	Workshop Staff
M/2	053747	A/Sergt.	Thaw W.	"
M/2	019546	A/Corpl.	Higgins J.E.	"
M/2	053878	Pte.	Anderson R.E.	"
M/2	053748	"	Atkinson G.	"
M/2	052951	"	Carter E.	"
M/2	050006	"	Graham T.	"
M/2	052977	"	Hullah E.	"
M/2	051032	"	Jowitt T.	"
M/2	052607	"	Pettitt B.A.E.	"
M/2	050500	"	Reece A.	"
M/1	05438	"	Steadman R.D.	"
M/2	053955	"	Ashton J.	Drivers
M/2	053769	"	Brown W.R.	"
M/2	053834	"	Chalmers J.	"
M/2	054551	"	Gregory H.	"
M/2	053970	"	Lowis G.	"
M/2	053896	"	Neale J.E.	"
M/2	053973	"	Smith P.	"
M/2	053978	"	Tysoe P.F.	"

19/12/15.

B.C. Barton Lieut.
O.C. 14th Divl. F.A.W.U.
M.T. A.S.C.

12ᵈ of J. A. W. U
Vol. 9

F 1

Jan 1916.

CONFIDENTIAL

WAR DIARY

OF

O.C. 14th Div. F.A.W.U.
MT. A.S.C.

From Jan 1st 1916 — To Jan 31st 1916.

(VOLUME 9.)

Army Form C. 2118.

WAR DIARY
or
INTELLIGENCE SUMMARY.
(Erase heading not required.)

Instructions regarding War Diaries and Intelligence
Summaries are contained in F. S. Regs., Part II.
and the Staff Manual respectively. Title pages
will be prepared in manuscript.

Place	Date	Hour	Summary of Events and Information	Remarks and references to Appendices
Nr Jean Abelon	Jan. 1	8 p.m.	1 Car awaiting spare parts. 4 cars & 1 m/cycle in for repair. 1 Fitter from Base M.T. Depot.	D.R.S.
"	2	9 p.m.	" " " " 3 " " 2 " " " "	S.R.S.
"	3	8 p.m.	" " " " 5 " " 3 " " " "	S.R.S.
"	4	10 p.m.	" " " " 10 Cars in for repair. Lorry to Vlamertinge to tow in car with broken back axle. Very heavy day. Raining	S.R.S.
"	5	9 p.m.	1 Car awaiting spare parts. 3 cars & 1 m/cycle in for repair.	S.R.S.
"	6	9 p.m.	" " " " 6 " " 1 " " " "	S.R.S.
"	7	9 p.m.	" 2 " " " 1 " " 3 " " " "	S.R.S.
"	8	10 p.m.	" 2 " " " 3 " " " " " "	S.R.S.
"	9	8 p.m.	" 2 " " " 5 " " 2 " " " "	S.R.S.
"	10	8 p.m.	" 3 " " " 3 " " 2 " " " "	S.R.S.
"	11	9 p.m.	" 2 " " " 4 " " " " " " 1 Fitter to Base M.T. Depot.	S.R.S.
"	12	9 p.m.	" 2 " " " 5 " " " " " "	S.R.S.
"	13	9 p.m.	" 2 " " " 3 " " 1 " " " "	S.R.S.
"	14	10 p.m.	" 2 " " " 3 " " 1 " " " " 1 Car to Railhead for despatch to S.H.Q.	S.R.S.
"	15	9 p.m.	" 3 " " " 6 " " 1 " " " "	S.R.S.

Army Form C. 2118.

WAR DIARY
or
INTELLIGENCE SUMMARY.
(Erase heading not required.)

Place	Date	Hour	Summary of Events and Information	Remarks and references to Appendices
McJean Maton	Jan 16	11 pm	3. Cars awaiting spare parts. 3 Cars & 3 M/cycles in for repair.	DCB
"	17	9 pm	3 " " " 2 " "	DCB
"	18	9 pm	3 " " " 2 " " Overhauling workshop engine	DCB
"	19	11 pm	3 " " " 3 " " "	DCB
"	20	8 pm	3 " " " 3 " " "	DCB
"	21	8 pm	3 " " " 2 " " "	DCB
"	22	8 pm	3 " " " 5 " " "	DCB
"	23	7 pm	3 " " " 2 " " "	DCB
"	24	9 pm	4 " " " 4 -3 " " "	DCB
"	25	9 pm	5 " " " 4 -1 " " "	DCB
"	26	10 pm	5 " " " 4 " " "	DCB
"	27	9 pm	5 " " " 4 " " "	DCB
"	28	9 pm	5 " " " 3 -1 " " "	DCB
"	29	10 pm	5 " " " 3 " " "	DCB
"	30	9 pm	15 " " " 5 Cars in for repair. Called out at 11 pm to bring in car with broken back axle at regimental Aid Post. Done difficulty in removing it before daylight.	DCB
"	31	8 pm	3 Cars awaiting spare parts. 4 cars under repair. 2 Cars to 3rd M.T. Repair Shop G.H.Q.	DCB

14 a. F.A.W.U.
Vol 10.

Feb 1916
March 1916

Confidential
War Diary
of
O.C. 14th Divl. F.A.W.U.
MT. A.S.C.

From Feb. 1st 1916   To Feb. 29th 1916.

(Volume. 10.)

Army Form C. 2118.

WAR DIARY
or
INTELLIGENCE SUMMARY.
(Erase heading not required.)

Instructions regarding War Diaries and Intelligence Summaries are contained in F. S. Regs., Part II. and the Staff Manual respectively. Title pages will be prepared in manuscript.

Place	Date	Hour	Summary of Events and Information	Remarks and references to Appendices
St Jean (Abeton)	Feb. 1	9 pm	1 car awaiting spare parts. 4 cars & 1 m/cycle for repair. 2 Ambulances to G.H.Q. Repair shops.	SES.
"	2	9 pm	" " " " 3 " " " "	BES.
"	3	10 pm	" " " " 4 " " " "	SES.
"	4	9 pm	" " " " 4 " " " "	SES.
"	5	9 pm	" " " " 1 " " " "	SES.
"	6	11 am	" " " " 2 " " " "	SES.
"	7	8 pm	1 " " " " 3 " " " " 4 Ambulances returned from G.H.Q. with necessary spare parts for repair. 1 damaged by bad towing.	SES.
"	8	9 pm	1 car awaiting spare parts. 9 cars & 2 m/cycles to repair	SES.
"	9	9 pm	9 cars in for repair. 1 Ambulance to G.H.Q. Repair shops.	SES.
"	10	10 pm	7 cars " " " Received orders from A.D.M.S. to march to Esquelbecq on 13-2-16.	SES.
"	11	9 am	6 " " " "	SES.
"	12	10 pm	" " " " Marched out at 9.30 am arrived Esquelbecq 11.30 am.	SES.
Esquelbecq	13	9 pm	2 " " " "	SES.
"	14	8.30 pm	2 " " " " & 2 m/cycles.	SES.
"	15	9 pm	3 " " " "	SES.

Army Form C. 2118.

WAR DIARY
or
INTELLIGENCE SUMMARY.
(Erase heading not required.)

Instructions regarding War Diaries and Intelligence Summaries are contained in F. S. Regs., Part II. and the Staff Manual respectively. Title pages will be prepared in manuscript.

Place	Date	Hour	Summary of Events and Information	Remarks and references to Appendices
Eaqueleep	16	9 p.m.	3 cars & 1 m/cycle for repair	A.D.S.
"	17	9 p.m.	2 " 1 " "	A.D.S.
"	18	9 p.m.	2 cars for repair. Received orders for A.D.M.S. to march out to Flesselles on 21-2-16.	A.D.S.
"	19	9 p.m.	3 cars & 5 m/cycles for repair	A.D.S.
"	20	9 p.m.	1 " & 1 " "	A.D.S.
Flesselles	21	11 a.m.	Marched at 7 am. and arrived Flesselles 5 pm.	A.D.S.
"	22	9 p.m.	1 car for repair	A.D.S.
"	23	9 p.m.	1 car for repair. Snow & Frost	A.D.S.
"	24	8 p.m.	1 " " " Heavy snowstorm.	A.D.S.
"	25	9 p.m.	Arrived all day on Treying had ?	A.D.S.
Doullens	26	9 p.m.	Marched at 9 am. arrived Doullens 10.45 am. 1 car for repair.	A.D.S.
"	27	9 p.m.	Awaiting orders to move up to Divl Arel.	A.D.S.
"	28	9 p.m.	" " "	A.D.S.
"	29	9 p.m.	" " "	A.D.S.

CONFIDENTIAL

WAR DIARY

OF

O. C. 14th Divl. F. A. W. U.
MT. A. S. C.

From March 1st 1916 — To March 31st 1916.

(VOLUME II.)

COMMITTEE FOR THE
MEDICAL HISTORY OF THE WAR

Date 9 - JUN. 1916

Army Form C. 2118.

WAR DIARY
INTELLIGENCE SUMMARY
(Erase heading not required.)

Instructions regarding War Diaries and Intelligence Summaries are contained in F.S. Regs., Part II. and the Staff Manual respectively. Title pages will be prepared in manuscript.

Place	Date	Hour	Summary of Events and Information	Remarks and references to Appendices
Doullens	March 1st	10 p.m.	Awaiting orders to move.	ses
Barly	2	9 a.m.	Moved to Barly. 2 Cars awaiting repair	ses.
"	3	9 p.m.	1 Car awaiting spare parts 2 cars & 2 m/cycles for repair	ses
"	4	8 p.m.	2 " " 3 " "	ses.
"	5	9 p.m.	2 " " 3 " "	ses.
"	6	9.30 p.m.	1 " " 1 " " 1 M/cycle to 14th Supply Column	ses.
"	7	10 p.m.	1 " " 2 " " 2 " " " "	ses
Foseux	8	10 p.m.	1 " " 2 " " Received orders for ADMS to proceed to Foseux on 8/3/16.	ses.
"	9	9 p.m.	1 " " 4 " " 1 Moved to Foseux	ses.
"	10	8 p.m.	1 " " 5 " " 1	ses.
"	11	9 p.m.	1 " " 4 " " 1.	ses
"	12	9 p.m.	1 " " 3 " " 1	ses
"	13	8 p.m.	1 " " 4 " " 2	ses
"	14	10 p.m.	1 " " 4 " " 1	ses
"	15	10 p.m.	1 " " 4 " " 2	ses
"	16	10 p.m.	1 " " 5 " " 1	ses.

Army Form C. 2118.

WAR DIARY
or
INTELLIGENCE SUMMARY.
(Erase heading not required.)

Instructions regarding War Diaries and Intelligence Summaries are contained in F. S. Regs., Part II. and the Staff Manual respectively. Title pages will be prepared in manuscript.

Place	Date	Hour	Summary of Events and Information		Remarks and references to Appendices
	March				
Fosseux	17	9 p.m	1. Car awaiting spare parts 3 cars in for repair		AEB
"	18	9 p.m	1 " " " " "		AEB
"	19	10 p.m	1 " " " " " Received orders for ADMS to proceed to WANQUETIN on 2/3/16		AEB
WANQUETIN	20	9 p.m	2 " " " " " Moved to WANQUETIN		BEB
"	21	9 p.m	1 " " " " " 1 car 1 on/cycle for repair		BEB
"	22	7:30 p.m	3 " " " " "		BEB
"	23	7:30 p.m	1 " " " " "		AEB
"	24	8 p.m	4 " " " " " 1 man sick to C.C.S. 1 man from Bow M.T. Depot		BEB
"	25	8 p.m	3 " " " " " "		AEB
"	26	7 p.m	2 " " 1 " " " and repairs to Foden disinfector		CEB
"	27	7 p.m	4 " " 1 " " " and repairs to 30 A.T. lorry		DEB
"	28	8 p.m	2 " " 1 " " "		REB
"	29	9 p.m	2 " " 2 " " "		REB
"	30	10 p.m	4 " " 1 " " " 1 Amb at divn from 3rd A.T.S.C.		BEB
"	31	11 p.m	3 " " 1 " " " 1 m/cycle to 14th Divn Supply Column		AEB

1577 Wt.W10791/1773 500,000 1/15 D.D.&L. A.D.S.S./Forms/C. 2118.

www.ingramcontent.com/pod-product-compliance
Lightning Source LLC
Chambersburg PA
CBHW081455160426
43193CB00013B/2492